Northwestern University
STUDIES IN *Phenomenology &*
Existential Philosophy

GENERAL EDITOR
John Wild

ASSOCIATE EDITOR
James M. Edie

CONSULTING EDITORS
Herbert Spiegelberg
William Earle
George A. Schrader
Maurice Natanson

In Praise of Philosophy

Maurice Merleau-Ponty

Translated, with a Preface by

In Praise of Philosophy

JOHN WILD &

JAMES M. EDIE

NORTHWESTERN UNIVERSITY PRESS

1963

Éloge de la Philosophie was delivered by Maurice
Merleau-Ponty as his Inaugural Lecture at the Collège
de France on January 15, 1953, and published by
Librairie Gallimard, Paris, in the same year.

Translation copyright © 1963 by Northwestern University Press

Library of Congress Catalog Card Number: 63–10500

Printed in the United States of America

ISBN 0-8101-0163-7

Third Printing, 1973

A Ma Mère

TRANSLATORS'

Preface

THIS TRANSLATION IS THE FIRST OF A SERIES
of publications which will be concerned with a new
way of thinking relevant to the situation and problems of our time. This current of thought is being
developed in different countries by thinkers of very
different backgrounds, and it goes by many different
names including *phenomenology* and *existential
philosophy*. In our own country, William James
called it *pragmatism*, and, later, *radical empiricism*,
and there is little question that he would feel very
much at home in this philosophical climate if he
were alive today. The Northwestern University Press
is undertaking the task of establishing this series of
publications with the aim of furthering work in
phenomenological and existential analysis among
American philosophers. The series will include both
translations of important works by European au-

thors and original studies by American philosophers.[1]

Those who have contributed to this living philosophy of our time include a wide variety of eminent names, such as Berdiaev in Russia; Ortega y Gasset in Spain; Sartre and Marcel in France; Husserl, Scheler, and Heidegger in Germany; and many others. These philosophers are free and independent thinkers who differ from one another in many ways. If we ask what it is, then, that enables us to bring them all under a common rubric, a cogent answer would at first seem to involve us in considerable difficulty. Nevertheless such an answer can be given. Put briefly, it comes to this: All these thinkers have been primarily concerned with the exploration of the original life-world, or *Lebenswelt,* as Husserl called it, into which we are born as men, in which we exist and pursue our chosen projects, and in which we face death. It is true that philosophers of the past have been aware of this primordial world. They have presupposed it and taken it for granted. But they have not deemed it worthy of their serious and disciplined attention as part of a cooperative inquiry. Rather, with only a few noteworthy exceptions, they have discounted it since the time of Plato as con-

1. Though it would be premature to list all the titles and manuscripts under consideration for publication in this series at the present time, we can announce the forthcoming publication of two other works by Merleau-Ponty: *Signes,* translated by Richard C. McCleary, and *Sens et non-sens,* translated by Hubert L. Dreyfus.

fused, unstable, and subjective, and have turned to other matters.

Indeed, it is true that this "world of the street," as James sometimes called it, is a vastly rich and far-ranging horizon and that we must take account of the conscious intentions around which it is centered as well as their concrete objects. It is also true that this world is not accessible to the highly abstract and selective methods of the natural sciences. As James said at the end of his *Varieties of Religious Experience,* "assuredly the real world is of a different temperament—more intricately built than science allows." [2] But from this it does not follow that its peculiar structures are not open to other methods and modes of understanding. The phenomenological thinkers listed above devoted their energies to the exploration of this life-world and to the implications of their findings for the different branches of philosophy and for the living issues of our time. This is also the interest of the editors, and any manuscript which makes a significant contribution to this common task will be eligible for publication in this series.

We believe that philosophy has a primary role to play in the disciplined fulfillment of this task. But we do not believe that it is restricted to academic philosophers alone. Already students of history, sociology, and anthropology, primitive religion, psy-

2. New York, Modern Library, 1955, p. 509.

chiatry, and other "human sciences" have made important contributions to this current of thought, and we see no reason why this interest should not be extended to the other humanistic disciplines. The philosophers we have mentioned all shared a deep concern for human freedom and responsibility, and they felt the need of grounding these concepts more profoundly in the roots of our historical, human existence. At the same time, they have all been able to learn from others embarked on the same common quest. We do not believe, therefore, that real participation in this cooperative endeavor can jeopardize in any way that spirit of criticism and independence which is so essential for authentic philosophy. We believe rather that authentic freedom will be elicited and that the meaning of philosophy itself will be clarified by this cooperation and interaction. In support of this we can offer the case of Merleau-Ponty himself.

He studied carefully not only Husserl's published works but also his *Nachlass* at Louvain. He was for a long time closely associated with Sartre and deeply influenced by him. He read widely in Scheler, as well as Heidegger, and was intimately familiar with the Gestalt psychology of the 1920's and 1930's. He took over insights from all these sources, but he became no man's disciple. He thought them through for himself and used them to support and to bring out further insights of his own. Nurtured on this ground, he made important contributions to the phenomeno-logical investigation of human existence in the life-world and its distinctive structures. We cannot help but think of him now as a free and independent, even a revolutionary thinker of our time, whose depth and originality was expressed not only in his words and writings but also in his life.

Maurice Merleau-Ponty died on May 4, 1961, still a young man, still a vigorous contributor to the age of philosophy which he had helped to create and to shape after the Second World War in France. He was a revolutionary, and his philosophy, even more than that of his French contemporaries, was a phi-losophy of the evolving, becoming *historical pres-ent.* In this sense his thought can never be a phi-losophy of the past, even though the duty of "threat-ening" other philosophers, of facing the crisis of life and thought in the second half of the twentieth cen-tury, has now devolved upon others.

While during his lifetime only a few pages of his writings were rendered into English, as incomplete and faulty samples, plans are now being made in various places for translations of his major works. The present translation of his Inaugural Lecture at the Collège de France is a harbinger of others to come. This lecture was delivered on January 15, 1953, after Merleau-Ponty had been elected to the chair of philosophy at the Collège de France—the youngest man ever to hold that chair. It was meant to serve as an introduction to the spirit and the main themes of his philosophy. Those who are not afraid of reading between the lines will find here all the principal themes of Merleau-Ponty on the philosophy of man and the life-world, of perception, language, history, and religion.

But this address was not delivered primarily to academic philosophers. It was addressed, rather, to the learned world as a whole, to all those who are "philosophers" in the higher sense of being preoccupied with what man has become, with the course of history, with the meaning and value of human life in the present. This duty of the philosopher to live among others and to dialogue with others who are not members of his closed corporation has, perhaps, been more a part of philosophy in France and other European countries than in our own universities. But Merleau-Ponty's sense of this duty of the philosopher is exceptional even for France, and we find in this Inaugural Lecture an attempt to express *what* the place of the philosopher is in the society of free men engaged in free research.

Merleau-Ponty, however, is not speaking to an audience of philosophical illiterates. No truly "free" man can be a philosophical illiterate. He addresses himself here to an audience of liberally educated men, not to tell them *about* philosophy or its results, but to *think through with them,* as philosophers, what the life of the philosopher is. "The philosopher" here is not Merleau-Ponty as opposed to those whom he is addressing; it is a name that belongs to all those engaged in exploring, on the frontiers of knowledge, the meaning of what it is to be, to perceive, to think, to speak, to act.

We have called Merleau-Ponty a philosopher of *the present,* but we do not mean by this that his philosophy is ephemeral. A philosopher can be *present to* his world in many different ways. In giving examples of the philosopher's "engagement" in the world and his *action* among and on his contemporaries, Merleau-Ponty recalls episodes from the lives of Spinoza, Lagneau, Bergson, Galileo, Descartes, and Socrates. The philosopher is a "man of action" of a special kind; he joins movements, he writes manifestoes, he engages in political activity but only in so far as he remains "free," not only to subject his action to critical reflexion but even to reject it altogether at the moment when it begins to go beyond its original intention, when it begins to "carry him along" with it into positions he did not intend. This is why the philosopher, in spite of his engagement, is always alone, never completely *of* a party or movement or an orthodoxy of any kind, though he may be *for* it while remaining outside it.

Merleau-Ponty is the philosopher who faced torture during the Resistance but who refused the *Légion d'Honneur,* who condemned the use of torture and the insubordination of the army in Algeria but who refused to sign the *Manifeste des 121*. We know that in *Sens et non-sens* he defended the political activity of Sartre and his group, whereas in *Les aventures de la dialectique* he subjected it, and by implication his own association with it, to a severe critique. Then, for a while, he retired into silence, not out of spite but because he had nothing further to say on this question for the moment. As action progresses, its meaning changes; we must always stand in readiness to re-assess the meaning we have given to history and to our lives. For Merleau-Ponty the most important activity of the philosopher is *thinking*, what he calls "radical reflection." Thus, even when he is most ardently engaged, there is always a distance between himself and the activity he supports, the *critical distance* of thinking through the meaning of his action. For "men of action" this kind of philosopher is an insupportable burden and a dangerous ally; they are rightly suspicious of him because he is never fully *with* them. For any orthodoxy the very fact that a man will think through its commands for himself, even though he obeys them, is a source of uneasiness; he always *could* rebel.

But Merleau-Ponty was a philosopher of *the present* in a more profound sense than in his intense moral and intellectual involvement with contemporary social and political events. The philosopher is the man who tries to "wake up," to become conscious and "to speak." But this effort at comprehension, at understanding himself and the world, does not dispense him from the human necessity of choosing and of acting without full knowledge. Merleau-Ponty views man as an essentially historical being and history as the dialectic of meaning and non-meaning which is working itself out through the complex, unpredictable interaction of men and the world. Nothing historical ever has just *one* meaning; meaning is ambiguous and is seen from an infinity of viewpoints. Everything is always *becoming* meaningful, and the task of the philosopher is to practice Socratic "doubt" and "irony," to probe, to test, to challenge the meanings which have been given to history in order that what it *means* may become clear. Merleau-Ponty has been called a philosopher of ambiguity, of contradiction, of dialectic. His search is the search for *meaning*.

He wrote *In Praise of Philosophy* without desiring to find or to assert any special privilege for the philosopher or to accord him any other dignity than that of being an honest man. His attempt to define the philosopher in history is an attempt to see himself in history and, then, to understand what this essentially historical existence of the philosopher, and therefore of man, is. He begins by situating his own thought with respect to that of his predecessors in the chair of philosophy at the Collège de

France: Bergson, Le Roy, and Lavelle.[3] In trying
to see and interpret these philosophers, and espe-
cially Bergson, as his "predecessors," Merleau-Ponty
is doing more than merely giving an *expositio re-
verentialis* of their doctrine. In order to give such an
exposition, one must first read and think what they
have said; having done this, it is no longer *their* doctrine but also *ours* which we must give. According to
Merleau-Ponty each generation must discover for
itself its own truth in the history of philosophy.
There is no "objective" truth of Bergson or of any
other philosopher, nor of human history as such.
The truth and meaning of Bergson's philosophy is

3. Some persons have wondered why Merleau-Ponty, in speaking of his predecessors at the Collège de France, does not men-
tion his most immediate "predecessor" in philosophy, Étienne
Gilson, who held the chair of the history of medieval philosophy
at the Collège de France from 1932–1950. Was this because
Gilson, member of the Légion d'Honneur and of the Académie
française, belonged to that generation of Sorbonne professors
against whom the contemporaries of Sartre and Merleau-Ponty
rebelled? Or was it because, by teaching only the history of
medieval philosophy, Gilson was not worthy of being taken into
account (cf. p. 41 of *In Praise of Philosophy* below)? There is
little evidence in his writings that Merleau-Ponty ever read Gilson in the way he read Bergson, Le Roy, and Lavelle. This is
unfortunate in that Gilson never considered his Thomism to be
anything less than a "contemporary" philosophy, and by passing
him over in silence Merleau-Ponty has deprived us of a con-
frontation of his own "existentialism" with the "Thomistic
existentialism" which Gilson represents and which he taught at
the Collège de France immediately after the war (cf. *L'Être et
l'essence*, Paris, 1948). Whatever the *meaning* of this silence on
the part of Merleau-Ponty, it is, no doubt, meant to be significant.

also a becoming, evolving truth. It is not a question of whether or not it is legitimate to understand Bergson from our own point in history and through our own thought, for if we are to read and understand him at all, this is the only point of view we have.

But though the philosopher has no access to a timeless truth outside of history and can never passively accept his own past, Merleau-Ponty shows us that this need not lead him into a relativism of isolated versions of the world, each fixed and closed within itself. In a society of free individuals who are able, within certain limits, to work out their own styles of life and versions of the world, it is a primary task of philosophy to elicit and to encourage a living communication between these versions and other worlds of the past. By fostering such communication, and by focusing the knots of lasting meaning which emerge from it, philosophy may help to make them more conscious of themselves as versions, and open them up to that one history and that one world which encompasses and yet transcends them all.

Merleau-Ponty felt that out of the investigations of phenomenology and existential thinking a new approach to the life-world was being formed and that on this basis a renewal and revival of philosophy at every level and in every branch was becoming possible. The editors share this view and its implicit hope for a strengthening of the humanistic disciplines on a new and more solid foundation. The natural sciences share a common field and a common method. The kind of truth to which they have access is generally understood and widely respected. This enables them to communicate, to cooperate, and to advance.

The humanistic disciplines, on the other hand, at the present time have little sense of a human world with distinctive structures of its own, or of a disciplined method for its exploration. Hence we find them exposed to the constant encroachment of alien methods and concepts taken from the different sciences and suffering from an inability to communicate, from the relativism that follows in its train, and from a general loss of nerve. But it is the merit of phenomenology to have disclosed the distinctively human world which has its own structures, which has to be understood in a different way, which is open to a different kind of confirmable truth. If this exploration of the life-world should take root and should be able to advance further, it could provide us with that foundation for the human disciplines of which the philosopher Dilthey dreamed at the end of the last century, and the lack of which brought about the "Crisis of the European Sciences" with which we are still confronted. Such a foundational study might make effective communication possible once again, and it might enable the human sciences to ward off the encroachments of alien methods and gain a deeper sense of their own autonomy and integrity.

It is with such considerations in mind that the editors have projected the series of "Studies in Phenomenology and Existential Philosophy" of which this is the first number. We feel that this small volume in which a well-known phenomenologist of our time, a philosopher who devoted a large part of his energies and talents to the painstaking and detailed analysis of life-structures, expresses his global vision of the historical world in which men live as "philosophers" is a fitting introduction to this series. We believe that this book and the volumes to be published subsequently are worthy of the attention of all those seriously concerned for the renewal of philosophy and for the strengthening of the humane disciplines.

JOHN WILD

JAMES M. EDIE

Northwestern University

September 13, 1962

Contents

In Praise of Philosophy

In Praise of Philosophy

Mister Provost, Colleagues, Ladies and Gentlemen:

The man who witnesses his own research, that
is to say his own inner disorder, cannot feel himself to be the heir of the distinguished men whose
names he sees on these walls.[1] If, in addition, he is
a philosopher, that is to say if he knows that he
knows nothing, how could he believe himself justified in occupying this chair, and how could he even
desire to do so? The answer to these questions is
very simple. Since its foundation the Collège de
France has been charged with the duty, not of giving
to its hearers already-acquired truths, but the idea
of free investigation. If, last winter, the Collège de
France desired to maintain a chair of philosophy,
it is because philosophical ignorance puts the crown-

1. This is the text of the inaugural lecture. Some notes which
were not read have been placed at the end of the volume

ing touch on the spirit of search to which it is devoted. If a philosopher solicits your votes, my dear colleagues, it is, you well know, in order to live the philosophical life more completely. And if you have elected him, it is to support this endeavor in his person. Although I feel unequal to the honor, I am nevertheless happy to undertake the task, since it is a great good fortune, as Stendhal said, for one "to have his passion as a profession." I have been touched at finding you so resolved, all other considerations aside, in desiring to maintain philosophy in your midst, and it is a pleasure to thank you for this today.

Without doubt I could not do better than to examine before you the function of the philosopher, first of all as it was exercised by my predecessors, and then as it pertains to this function to consider both the past of philosophy and its present.

I / Lavelle[2]

THE PHILOSOPHER IS MARKED by the distinguishing trait that he possesses *inseparably* the taste for evidence and the feeling for ambiguity. When he limits himself to accepting ambiguity, it is

2. For purposes of clarification the translators have added titles to the various sections of this lecture, and certain long paragraphs have been divided.

called equivocation. But among the great it becomes a theme; it contributes to establishing certitudes rather than menacing them. Therefore it is necessary to distinguish good and bad ambiguity. Even those who have desired to work out a completely positive philosophy have been philosophers only to the extent that, at the same time, they have refused the right to install themselves in absolute knowledge. They taught not this knowledge, but its becoming in us, not the absolute but, at most, our *absolute relation* to it, as Kierkegaard said. What makes a philosopher is the movement which leads back without ceasing from knowledge to ignorance, from ignorance to knowledge, and a kind of rest in this movement.

Even conceptions as limpid as those which M. Lavelle so deliberately oriented toward pure being would verify this definition of the philosopher. Lavelle gave as the object of philosophy "this whole of being in which our own existence is being inscribed by a continuous miracle." He spoke of a miracle because there is a paradox here: the paradox of a total being which is, in advance, everything which we can be and do, and yet which would not be it without us, and which thus needs to be augmented by our own being. Our relation with being involves a double sense, the first according to which we belong to it, the second according to which it belongs to us. We cannot, therefore, place ourselves in being in order to derive ourselves and the world from it. If we do this, it is only possible, says Lavelle, "by dissimulating that both are already known." My situation in the world before any reflexion, and my initiation into existence cannot be reabsorbed by the reflexion which goes beyond them towards the absolute, nor can they be treated afterwards as effects. The movement by which we go from ourselves towards the absolute continually underlies the descending movement which detached thought accomplishes by going from the absolute towards itself. In fact, what the philosopher poses is never absolutely absolute; it is the absolute with respect to him. With these ideas of participation and presence, Lavelle rightly tried to define a relationship between ourselves and total being which always remains reciprocal to some extent.

His works thus had to develop on two sides. First of all, the world, that profound treasure in which the naive man thinks he discovers the primordial meaning of being, appears to Lavelle without depth and without mystery. It is the *phenomenon*, that which appears and has no interior. We could not have learned the meaning of the word "being" merely by considering this scenery. It is in ourselves and only in ourselves that we can touch the interior of being, because it is only there that we discover a being which has an interior and which is nothing but this interior. There is thus no transitive relation between me and my body, me and the world, and it is only "towards the within" that the self can overflow. My only commerce is with a perfect interiority, the model (but also, we shall see, the copy) of the imperfect interiority which defines me. Meditation on being is localized in the *self* and in *the more myself than myself*, behind the world and history. From this point of view philosophy has scarcely any problems or anything to do. Its sole task is to remind men of a participation in universal being which they could never completely forget without ceasing to be, and which, in the words of the preface to *Présence totale*, has always been entrusted to the *philosophia perennis*. Hence the philosopher has nothing to do in history, or in the debates of his period. Prefacing a book of political philosophy, Lavelle wrote that spiritual reform will reform the state "without anyone having had to think about it."

Then there is the other side. An infinite ego is not an *I*. For Lavelle only a being who suffers can say *I*. Thus I do not have a true knowledge of God through myself. It is only by carrying himself beyond himself, by faith, that the philosopher can pose God, says Lavelle, and for this very reason he can never think from the point of view of God. There is a truth of the world and of thought according to the world. For it, God is "the infinite Solitary, the perfectly Separated,

the eternally Absent," says Lavelle. And it is because
God is inaccessible to us, and without ever ceasing
to be inaccessible, that he becomes present to our
own solitude and our own separation. Thus our relation to being, which was thought to be entirely positive, is now hollowed out with a double negation.
And the result is that, in order to pose itself, this
relation has need of the world which but a minute
ago was only an appearance. The visible evidence of
interiority now reassumes its importance; it is not
a borrowed garment but the incarnation of interiority. Thought without language, says Lavelle, would
not be a purer thought; it would be no more than the
intention to think. And his last book offers a theory of
expressiveness which makes of expression not "a
faithful image of an already realized interior being,
but the very means by which it is realized." The sensible and the phenomenon, he continues, not only
limit our participation in being; "we incorporate
them into the positive essence of each being in such
a way that we can say, if not that being is only what
appears, it is at least that by which it appears." Here
there is no longer any alternative between the phenomenon, or matter, and being, or the spirit. True
spiritualism, writes Lavelle, consists in rejecting the
alternatives of spiritualism and materialism. Philosophy thus cannot consist in turning our attention
from matter to the spirit or complete itself in the
non-temporal affirmation of a non-temporal interior-

ity. There is, says Lavelle, only "the philosophy of to-day, that which I can think and live now."[3]

At the bottom of Lavelle's thought, perhaps, lay the idea that the unfolding of time and the world is the same thing as their consummation in the past. But this also means that one does not go beyond the world except by entering into it and that the spirit makes use of the world, time, speech, and history in a single movement and animates them with a meaning which is never used up. It would be the function of philosophy, then, to record this passage of meaning rather than to take it as an accomplished fact. Lavelle never says this. But it seems to us that his idea of a central function of the temporal present turned him away from a retrospective philosophy which would convert the world and history into a universal past in advance.

II / Bergson

IT IS IN THIS POINT of the present that Lavelle's descending dialectic crossed the ascending dialectic of Bergson and Le Roy. We name them together in spite of the differences which we will emphasize later, because their ideas should no more be separated in what we say of them than they were meant to be in their development. Bergson and Le

3. See Note I at the end of the volume.

Roy began from the world and constituted time. But they arrived at what inwardly animates world and time, at what Bergson called the *hesitation of time* and what Le Roy called *invention*. They reached, on its temporal side, the same joining of happening and meaning which preoccupied the later Lavelle, and we find at this point in their research the same ambiguous sparkle.

What we are saying here is discovered only after one has gone beyond the first appearance of Bergsonism. For there is even in Bergson a completely positive way of presenting the intuition of the *durée,* of matter, of life, and of God. Is not the discovery of the *durée* at first the discovery of a second reality in which the instant at the very moment of its passage maintains itself, conserves itself undivided in the present, and grows? Is not the *durée* a kind of flowing thing which remains while it melts away? And do not the later studies of Bergson consist in rediscovering in *other things,* in matter, in life, the same real cohesion at first disclosed in us? The last pages of *Matter and Memory* speak of a "presentiment" and of an "imitation" of memory in matter. *Creative Evolution* attaches life, in the terms of Bergson, "either to consciousness itself, or to something that resembles it." And how could something resemble consciousness if the consciousness we are thinking of does not already have the fullness of a thing? At times Bergson treats of consciousness as a substance spread out through the universe, which in rudimentary organisms is "compressed in a kind of vise" and which in those more differentiated organisms is allowed to develop. What then is this "large current of consciousness," without organism, without individuality, which Bergson says runs through matter? Viewed as a cosmological factor, consciousness is unrecognizable. When Bergson later on expressly identifies it with God, it is difficult to recognize an ego in this "center from which all worlds spring forth like the stems of an immense bouquet." It is the God of mystical experience who in the *Two Sources* definitively gives personality to cosmological consciousness. But even then the Bergsonian God remains very different from anything we can call thought or will because it excludes the negative component. Divine thought or will, says Bergson, is "too full of itself" for us to find in it the idea of non-being. "This would be a weakness incompatible with its nature, which is force." Held between the two Powers, God, who is force, and life, which is action, man, as he is, can only appear as a failure. He is the phantom of a "divine humanity" which, says Bergson, "should have existed theoretically from the beginning," and history, the communicative life of men, is not an autonomous order. It oscillates between the frenzy of action and mysticism; it is not in this history that we will find the guiding thread.

Fullness of the *durée,* primordial fullness of

cosmological consciousness, fullness of God, these results imply a theory of intuition as coincidence or
contact. And in fact Bergson defined philosophy as a
"semi-divine" state in which all the problems which
"put us in the presence of emptiness" are ignored.
Why have I been born? Why is there something
rather than nothing? How can I know anything?
These traditional questions are "pathological" for
Bergson, like those of the doubter who no longer
knows whether he has closed the window. They only
appear when we try to place ourselves intellectually
in a primordial emptiness, whereas emptiness, non-
being, nothingness, disorder are never anything
other than a purely verbal way of saying that we ex-
pected something else, and thus they presuppose a
subject already installed in being. Philosophy, true
thought, which is entirely positive, will rediscover
this naive contact already presupposed in the apparatus of negation and language in general. This
true thought Bergson frequently calls "fusion" with
things or "inscription," "recording," "impression" of
things in us. It seeks less to "resolve" classical problems than to "dissolve" them. "Simple act," "viewing
without a point of view," direct access without interposed symbols to the interior of things—all these
celebrated formulas of intuition define it as a massive grip on being, without exploration, without interior movement of meaning.

This is an aspect of Bergsonism which is the easiest to see. But it is not the only one, nor the most valid. For these formulas express less what Bergson had to say than his break with received doctrine at the time he began his research. [It is said that he restored intuition against the intellect and logic, spirit against matter, life against mechanism.] This is how both his friends and his adversaries understood him when his studies appeared. But his adversaries have missed the point. Perhaps it is time to look in Bergson for something more than the antithesis to their abandoned theses. In spite of the paradox, the wholly positive Bergson is a polemic writer, and as the negative begins to reappear in his philosophy, it is progressively affirmed. It would perhaps show more attention to his writings if we were to look in them for his views on the living and difficult relations of the spirit with the body and the world, rather than for the critique of Taine and Spencer; to look for the interior movement which animates his intuitions, which ties them to one another, and which frequently reverses their initial relationships, rather than for successive assertions. In this way Bergson would be truly delivered from his adversaries, delivered also from his "friends" who, as Péguy has already said, understood him no better. And we would recognize at the same time the soundness of studies like those of Le Roy, which never stop at Bergsonian positivism but which, on essential points like the theory of intuition and of the immediate and the limit, give Bergsonism its most authentic interpretation.

Bergson wanted to be finished with traditional problems, not to eliminate the problematic of philosophy but to revivify it. He saw so clearly that all philosophy must be, in the words of Le Roy, a new philosophy, that it is so little the discovery of a solution inscribed in being which satisfies our curiosity, that he demands of it not only the invention of solutions but the invention of its own problems. In 1935 he wrote: "I call an *amateur* in philosophy anyone who accepts the terms of a usual problem as they are . . . doing philosophy authentically would consist in *creating* the framework of the problem and of *creating* the solution." Thus when he says that well-posed problems are very close to being solved, this does not mean that we have already *found* what we are looking for, but that we have already invented it. It is not that there would be a question in us and a response in things, an exterior being to be discovered by an observing consciousness; the solution is also in us, and being itself is problematic. Something of the nature of the question passes into the answer.

The famous Bergsonian coincidence certainly does not mean, then, that the philosopher loses himself or is absorbed into being. [We must say rather that he experiences himself as transcended by being.] It is not necessary for him to go outside himself in order to reach the things themselves; he is solicited or haunted by them from within. For an ego which is *durée* cannot grasp another being except in the form of another *durée*. By experiencing my own manner of using up time, I grasp it, says Bergson, as a "choice among an infinity of possible *durées*." There is a "singular nature" of the *durée* which makes it at once my manner of being and a universal dimension for other beings in such a way that what is "superior" and "inferior" to us still remains "in a certain sense, interior to us." What I observe is a concordance and a discordance of things with my *durée;* these are the things with me in a lateral relationship of coexistence. I have the idea of a *durée* of the universe distinct from mine only because it extends the whole length of mine and because it is necessary that something in the melting sugar respond to my waiting for a glass of sugar water. When we are at the source of the *durée,* we are also at the heart of things because they are the adversity which makes us wait. The relation of the philosopher to being is not the frontal relation of the spectator to the spectacle; it is a kind of complicity, an oblique and clandestine relationship. We understand now how Bergson can say that the absolute is "very close to us and, in a certain measure, in us." It is in the way in which things modulate our *durée.*

If to do philosophy is to discover the primary sense of being, then one does not philosophize in quitting the human situation; it is necessary rather to plunge into it. The absolute knowledge of the philosopher is perception. "Suppose," says the first Oxford Conference, "that instead of wishing to elevate ourselves above our perception of things, we immerse ourselves in it in order to bore into this perception and enlarge it . . . , we would have a philosophy to which it would be impossible to oppose others, because it would not have left anything outside itself which other doctrines could pick up; it would have taken everything." [Perception grounds everything because it shows us, so to speak, an obsessional relation with being; it is there before us, and yet it touches us from within.] "Whatever the intimate essence of that which is and of that which happens may be," says Bergson, "we are of it." Perhaps he did not understand the full meaning of these words. We can see here an allusion to an objective evolution which brings man out of animality, the animal from cosmological consciousness, cosmological consciousness from God, and which would have left some sediments in us. Philosophy would in that case consist in dating these sediments. It would be a cosmological construction. Consciousness would look for its ancestors in things; it would project into them souls or analogues of souls; philosophy would be a panpsychism. But, since Bergson says that it is a generalized perception, it is in actual and present perception, not in some now completed genesis, that it is necessary to search for the relationship of our being with things.

"We are of it" thus means that these colors, these objects which we see, decorate and inhabit even our dreams, that these animals are humorous variants of ourselves, that all beings are symbolic of our life, and that this is what we see in them. Matter, life, God are not "interior" to us, as Bergson says, if by "matter" we mean the matter in itself which appeared one day through a kind of failing of the transcendent principle; if by "life" we mean life in itself, that feeble movement which once upon a time palpitated in a little newly made protoplasm; if by "God" we mean God in himself, the "immense" force which hangs over us. It can only be a question of matter, of life, of God in so far as they are perceived by us. The genesis which the works of Bergson trace is a history of ourselves which we tell to ourselves; it is a natural myth by which we express our ability to get along with all the forms of being. We are not this pebble, but when we look at it, it awakens resonances in our perceptive apparatus; our perception appears to come from it. That is to say our perception of the pebble is a kind of promotion to (conscious) existence for itself; it is our recovery of this mute thing which, from the time it enters our life, begins to unfold its implicit being, which is revealed to itself through us. What we believed to be coincidence is coexistence.

Perhaps Bergson began by understanding philosophy as a simple return to what is *given,* but later on he saw that this secondary, laborious, rediscovered naiveté does not merge us with a previous reality, does not identify us with the thing itself, without any point of view, without symbol, without perspective. Formulas like "sounding," "auscultation," "palpation," which are better, make it sufficiently clear that intuition needs to be understood, that it is necessary for me to appropriate to myself a meaning in it which is still captive. What precisely is intuitive in intuition? Bergson admits that most of the time it is present to the philosopher only in the form of a certain "power of negation" that excludes theses which are insufficient. Should we suppose a positive and already made view which underlies these negative appearances and sustains them? This would be to give way to the retrospective illusion, precisely criticized by Bergson. The global view which he calls intuition orients the whole effort of expression of the philosopher, but it does not contain it in abridged form. We would be wrong in imagining in Berkeley, before he thought or wrote, an abridged Berkeley which would have contained his whole philosophy and more. We would be wrong in believing, though Bergson said so, that the philosopher speaks all his life *for want of* being able to say this "infinitely simple thing" forever concentrated "in a single point" of himself. He also speaks *to say it,* because it demands to be said, because it is not achieved before it has been said. It is perfectly true that each philosopher, each painter, considers what the others call his work as the simple rough sketch of a work which still remains to be done. This does not prove that this work exists somewhere within themselves and they have only to lift a veil to reach it.

M. Gueroult showed in this very place last year that the secret and the center of a philosophy does not lie in a prenatal inspiration, but that it develops as the work progresses, that it is a becoming-meaning, which builds itself in accord with itself and in reaction against itself, that a philosophy is necessarily a (philosophical) history, an exchange between problems and solutions in which each partial solution transforms the initial problem in such wise that the meaning of the whole does not pre-exist it, except as a style pre-exists its works, and seems, after the fact, to announce them. What Gueroult says here of intuition applied to philosophical systems, we can say in general of philosophical intuition, and this time with Bergson's consent. It is proper to intuition to call forth a development, to become what it is, because it contains a double reference to the mute being which it interrogates, and to the tractable [*maniable*] meaning which is derived from it. It is the experience of their concordance; it is, as Bergson happily said, a *reading*, the art of grasping a meaning in a style before it has been put into concepts. And finally *the thing itself* is the virtual focal point of these convergent formulations.

The more energetic our intention to see the things themselves, the more the appearances by which they are expressed and the words by which we express them will be interposed between these things and us. In the very measure to which Bergson succeeded in showing that emptiness, nothingness, or disorder is never in things, that there are, outside of us, only presences, he came to designate ubiquity as the fundamental property of our spirit, the power of being elsewhere and of aiming at being only indirectly and obliquely. He says very well that the spirit "refuses to keep its place and concentrates all its attention on this refusal; it never determines its actual position except with respect to the one it has just left, like a passenger at the rear of a train who sees only the places he has left behind." Are we not always in the position of this traveler? Are we ever at the point of objective space which our body occupies? Is not our insertion in space always indirect, reflected towards us by the perspectival aspect of things which indicates the location which *should* be ours? In order to be able to treat this indirect relation and this distance with respect to being as a bad habit of the practical intellect, it is necessary to expel non-being from the world and, then, from ourselves.

Bergson thought he had done this by showing

that a nothingness in consciousness would be the consciousness of a nothingness, and that it would, therefore, not be nothing. But this is to say in other words that the being of consciousness is made of a substance so subtle that it is not less consciousness in the consciousness of an emptiness than in that of a thing. The primary being with respect to nothingness is thus not the natural or positive being of things; it is, Bergson himself says, existence in a Kantian sense, radical contingency. And if true philosophy dispels the vertigo and the anxiety that come from the idea of nothingness, it is because it interiorizes them, because it incorporates them into being and conserves them in the vibration of the being which is becoming. "If we refuse the intuition of emptiness," wrote M. Bachelard, "we have the right to refuse the intuition of fullness . . . This is as much as to say that, after various transpositions, we find the fundamental dialectic of being and nothingness stretched out in time. We thus give Bergson's formula its full ontological and temporal meaning: time is hesitation."

Le Roy turned Bergsonism away from a massive realism a long time ago. For him intuition is a "colored moment of the *cogito*," that is to say, a *cogito* which does not only render me certain, in the restrictive sense, of *my* thought, but also of what responds to it in the singular aspect of each thing. It is the experience of a thought which is sleeping in things and which is awakened at the approach of my thought. For Le Roy the famous "images" of the first chapter of *Matter and Memory* become, in his own words, "the lightning-flash of existence," the point at which I make the real "gleam" and reveal itself. Immediate experience is what awakens in me this fundamental phenomenon and what changes the "wholeness of its object into a group of living operations." When known being coincides with being, it is not because it fuses with it. Being is for the intuition a limit in the true sense of the word, that is to say, according to Le Roy, "a certain style of movement immanent in the very succession of stages, a certain quality of progression discernible by intrinsic comparisons," a "converging character" of the series. Thus Le Roy gave intuition a component of negativity and ambiguity without which it would be blind.

To get a true idea of Bergsonism it would now be necessary to take up his fundamental intuitions one by one and show how the initial positivism is transcended in each of them. Jean Hyppolite has recently begun this work in so far as it concerns the intuition of the *durée*. He has shown that the *durée* of the *Essay on the Immediate Data of Consciousness,* the undividedness of the interior life which is preserved whole, becomes, in *Matter and Memory*, a system of oppositions between the emptiness of the past, the emptiness of the future, and the fullness of the present, like the oppositions between time and

space. The very nature of the *durée* now requires
that it be internally divided into these three dimen-
sions and that it receive in itself the body and spa-
tiality which constitute the present and without
which even the past would remain nebulous and
would not be evoked, that is to say recovered and expressed. Henceforth the spirit is no longer undividedness; it is what "strives to gather itself together," as Hyppolite says, between the two limits of
pure memory and pure action, which are synonyms
of unconsciousness.[4]

One could note an analogous movement in the intuition of life. There are moments in which it is no
longer the fusion of the philosopher with a consciousness in things, but the consciousness of an
agreement between itself and the phenomena. Then
it is no longer a question of explaining life but of de-
ciphering it, says Bergson, as a painter deciphers a
face. It is necessary to rediscover "the intention of
life, the simple movement which runs through the
lines, which ties them to one another and gives
them a meaning." We are capable of this kind of
reading because we carry in our incarnate being the
alphabet and the grammar of life, but this does not
presuppose an achieved meaning either in us or in
it.[5] Here again Le Roy resolutely followed the better
direction of Bergsonism when he defined life as a

4. See Note II at the end of the volume.
5. See Note III at the end of the volume.

"groping finality," in which end and means, meaning and chance call forth one another. We do not recognize in this pregnant finality, in this meaning in labor, the sovereign ease of the cosmological consciousness which lets fall out of itself, with a simple gesture, like a movement of our hand, all the details that constitute the life of an organism.

For even greater reason it is necessary to ask if the intuition of God in Bergson is summed up in the God "who is force," of which we have spoken above. We know that he briefly defined the being of God as a *durée* that is more *durée* than our own. It is, he says, the "concentration" of every *durée*, and he calls it the "eternity of life," which *eminently* contains our *durée*. But this is to say that, in going from God to us, we go from the greater to the lesser, and that this lesser does not need explanation, since nothingness, as Malebranche said, has no properties. But we have just seen Bergson ultimately define our *durée* by the double nothingness which the future and the past oppose to the present, by a break in the fullness of being. If God is truly eternity of life, if, as Bergson says, "he is not at all fully realized," it is necessary that negativity penetrate the God "who is force." Is it enough to say here what Bergson puts in the mouth of Ravaisson, that "infinite Thought has annulled something of the plenitude of its being in order to take from it, by a kind of awakening and resurrection, everything which exists"? But if God really broke himself open in order to install the negative within himself, and if beings only appear in the opposite movement of change, they do not proceed from him. He is not a principle from which we can descend towards our *durée* and the world; he is a God towards whom we climb, whom the *durée* divines at each moment of its growth—as we sense an imminent phantasm at the edge of our visual field—but which cannot be *fixed*, cannot be known, and which cannot be independent of it and for itself.

This is even more striking in what Bergson says of God as the principle of the good. We know that he energetically rejected the arguments of classical theodicy which make evil a lesser good. "The philosopher," he says, "can content himself with arguments of this kind in the silence of his office. What will he think of them before a mother who has just seen her child die?" The only optimism he admits is an "empirical" optimism: the fact is that men, in spite of everything, accept life, and also there is a joy beyond pleasure and pain. This optimism does not *justify* suffering by joy, as its condition. It presupposes nothing like an infinite regard which, penetrating the world and the obscurity of suffering through and through, would be the equivalent of an approbation. Everything happens, according to Bergson, as if man encountered at the roots of his constituted being a generosity which is not a compromise with the adversity of the world and which is on his side against it. In rejecting the idea of God as a theoretical explanation, Le Roy says the same thing more energetically: ". . . We know God by his very life in us, in the work of our deification. In this sense we can even say that, for us, God is not, but that he is becoming." There is in Bergsonian theology, as perhaps in every theology since Christianity, an ambiguity thanks to which we never know if it is God who sustains men in their human being or if it is the inverse, since in order to know his existence it is necessary to pass through ours, and this is not an optional detour.

With respect to God who is force, our existence was a failure and the world a decadence which we could not heal except by returning here below. To the God who is on the side of men corresponds, on the contrary, a forward-looking history which is an experience searching for its accomplishment. Bergson's critique of the idea of progress aims at a progress without contingency, which would happen of itself. That is a particular case of the retrospective illusion. We see in a happening of the past the preparation of our present, whereas this past was "a complete act" in its time and it is the present success which transforms it into a rough design. But this underlines precisely the strange power we have of reviving the past, of inventing a sequel for it. Even if there is a metamorphosis here, it would not take place without a common meaning of the past and of the present. Bergson thus admits a sense of history as it develops and a progress, on condition that this is not a force which would act of itself, but which would be understood as something more to be made than observed, defined not by an *idea* but by a constant *orientation*. Granted this, there is nothing in history that is completely without meaning. Its dichotomies, its impasses, its returnings to abandoned paths, its discords have the appearance of non-sense only for an abstract mind which would reduce the problems of history to the problems of ideas.

But it is not merely a question here of confronting ideas but of incarnating them and of making them live, and in this respect we cannot know what they are capable of except by trying them out. This attempt involves a taking of sides and a struggle. The struggle here, says Bergson, is thus only "the superficial aspect of progress." It is well that the primordial unity was broken in order that the world and history might take place. The discord of man with himself, which up to now impeded him from being the "divine man," now constitutes his reality and his value. He is divided because he is not a "species" or a "created thing," because he is a "creative effort." He is a "realized contradiction," Bergson says, because humanity cannot validly "constitute itself ultimately without the aid of man himself." The undividedness of the origins is a symbol which our present will to be gives as both body and mind. It is

the invitation to create out of nothing a body of institutions in which the spirit can recognize itself.
Hence Bergson's unconservative tone, whether it is
a question of machinism, leisure for the working-
man, or the status of women. On this point also Le
Roy anticipated the latent sense of Bergsonism when
he spoke of our whole history as a revolution that
has been developing since the Renaissance and when
he spoke of the "absolute value of humanization"
[*hominisation*].

We can summarize the internal movement of
Bergsonism by saying that it is the development
from a philosophy of impression to a philosophy of
expression. What Bergson said against language has
caused us to forget what he said in its favor. There
is the language frozen on paper or in discontinuous
elements in space, and there is the living word, the
equal and the rival of thought, as Valéry said. Bergson saw this. If man arises in the midst of the world
and transforms the automatisms of nature, he owes
it, according to Bergson, to his body, to his brain: "he
owes it to his language which furnishes consciousness with an immaterial body in which it can incarnate itself." In and through language it is generally
the expression with which Bergson is concerned. He
saw that philosophy did not consist in realizing freedom and matter, spirit and body apart from one another or in opposing them. In order to be themselves,
freedom and spirit must witness themselves in mat-

ter or in the body; that is to say, they must express themselves. "It is a question," he says in *Creative Evolution*, "of creating with matter, which is pure necessity, an instrument of freedom, of fabricating a mechanism which will triumph over mechanism." Matter is an obstacle, but it is also an instrument and a stimulus. It is as if the spirit which, from the beginning, hovered over the waters had need of constructing for itself the instruments of its manifestation in order to exist completely.

⌊What we call expression is only another formula for the phenomenon to which Bergson continually returns—the retroactive effect of the true.⌉ The experience of the true cannot keep from projecting itself back into the time which preceded it. Frequently this is only an anachronism and an *illusion*. But in *Thought and Movement* Bergson suggests, in speaking of a *retrograde movement of the true,* that it is a question of a fundamental property of truth. To think, or, in other words, to think an idea as true, implies that we arrogate to ourselves the right of recovering the past, either to treat it as an anticipation of the present, or at least to place the past and the present in the same world. What I say of the sensible world is not in the sensible world, and yet it has no other meaning than to say what the sensible world means. The expression antedates itself and postulates that being comes towards it. This exchange between the past and the present, between matter and

[margin annotation: Lived Experience Embodiment]

spirit, silence and speech, the world and us, this metamorphosis of one into the other, with a transparent gleam of truth, is, in our view, much more than the famous intuitive coincidence, the best of Bergsonism.

A philosophy of this kind understands its own strangeness, for it is never entirely in the world, and yet never outside the world. Expression presupposes someone who expresses, a truth which he expresses, and the others before whom he expresses himself. The postulate of expression and of philosophy is that it can simultaneously satisfy these three conditions. Philosophy cannot be a tête-à-tête of the philosopher with the true. It cannot be a judgment given from on high on life, the world, history, as if the philosopher *was not part of it*—nor can it subordinate the internally recognized truth to any exterior instance of it. It must go beyond this alternative.

Bergson understood this well. After declaring in his testament of 1937 that his reflexions had "led him closer and closer to catholicism," he added these words which pose our problem: "I would have been converted if I had not seen for many years the beginnings of the fearsome wave of antisemitism which was about to break out in the world. I have wished to remain among those who tomorrow will be the persecuted." We know that he kept his word even to the point of refusing, in spite of sickness and age, the favors which a power, ashamed of its own principles, wanted to give to this illustrious Jew. Therefore no secret baptism, in spite of the legend, and in spite of his assent on fundamentals. It is here that we see how Bergson conceived our relation to truth. The assent to truths borne by an institution or a church could not release him from this pact of history which he had made with the persecuted of tomorrow. His conversion would have been a desertion, and an open adherence to Christianity could not prevail over the God who was hidden in the sufferings of the persecuted.

We can say: if the philosopher truly thinks that a church holds the secrets of life and the instruments of salvation, he cannot better serve others than by serving it without reservations. But this is doubtless a vain hypothesis. By the very choice he made, Bergson attested that, for him, there is no *place of truth* to which one should go to search for it at any cost, even breaking human relationships and the ties of life and history. Our relationship to the true passes through others. Either we go towards the true with them, or it is not towards the true that we are going. But the real difficulty is that, if the true is not an idol, the others in their turn are not gods. There is no truth without them, but it does not suffice to attain to the truth to be with them. At the time when he was being earnestly asked finally to write his ethics, Bergson wrote a little phrase which shows this well: "one is never obliged to write a book." We cannot ex-

pect a philosopher to go beyond what he sees himself, or to give precepts of which he is not sure. The
impatience of others is not an argument here; one
does not serve others by the more-or-less or by im-
posture. Thus it is the philosopher and he alone who
is judge.

Here we have come back to the self and to the
tête-à-tête of the self with the true. Now we have
said that there is no solitary truth. Are we therefore
on a revolving wheel? We are, but it is not the wheel
of the skeptics. It is true that in the last resort there
is no judge, that I do not think according to the true
alone, nor according to myself alone, nor according
to the others alone, because each of the three has
need of the other two and it would be a non-sense to
sacrifice any one. A philosophical life always bases
itself on these three cardinal points. The enigma of
philosophy (and of expression) is that sometimes
life is the same to oneself, to others, and to the true.
These are the moments which justify it. The philosopher counts only on them. He will never accept to
will himself against men, nor to will men against
himself, nor against the true, nor the true against
them. He wishes to be everywhere at once, at the
risk of never being completely anywhere. His opposition is not aggressive; he knows that this often an-
nounces capitulation. But he understands the rights
of others and of the outside too well to permit them
any infringement. If, when he is engaged in external

enterprises, the attempt is made to draw him beyond the point where his activity loses the meaning which inspired it, his rejection is all the more tranquil in that it is founded on the same motives as his acceptance. Hence the rebellious gentleness, the pensive engagement, the intangible presence which disquiet those who are with him. As Bergson said of Ravaisson in a tone so personal that one imagines him to be speaking of himself: "He gave no hold. . . . He was the kind of man who does not even offer sufficient resistance for one to flatter himself that he has ever seen him give way."

III / Socrates

IF WE HAVE RECALLED these words of Bergson, not all of which are in his books, it is because they make us feel that there is a tension in the relation of the philosopher with other persons or with life, and that this uneasiness is essential to philosophy. We have forgotten this a little. The modern philosopher is frequently a functionary, always a writer, and the freedom allowed him in his books admits an opposite view. What he says enters first of all into an academic world where the choices of life are deadened and the occasions for thought are cut off. Without books a certain speed of communication would be impossible, and there is nothing to say against them.

But in the end they are only words expressed a bit more coherently. The philosophy placed in books has ceased to challenge men. What is unusual and almost insupportable in it is hidden in the respectable life of the great philosophical systems. In order to understand the total function of the philosopher, we must remember that even the philosophical writers whom we read and who we are have never ceased to recognize as their patron a man who never wrote, who never taught, at least in any official chair, who talked with anyone he met on the street, and who had certain difficulties with public opinion and with the public powers. We must remember Socrates.

The life and death of Socrates are the history of the difficult relations that the philosopher faces—when he is not protected by literary immunity—with the gods of the City, that is to say with other men, and with the fixed absolute whose image they extend to him. If the philosopher were a rebel, it would be less shocking. For in the last analysis each one of us knows for his own part that the world as it is, is unacceptable. We like to have this written down for the honor of humanity, though we may forget it when we return to our affairs. Hence rebellion is not displeasing. But with Socrates it is something different. He teaches that religion is true, and he offered sacrifices to the gods. He teaches that one ought to obey the City, and he obeys it from the very beginning to the end. He is reproached not so much for what he does as for his way of doing it, his motive. In the *Apology* there is a saying which explains it all, when Socrates says to his judges: *Athenians, I believe as none of those who accuse me.* Revealing words! [He believes *more* than they, but also he believes in another way, and in a different sense.] True religion for Socrates is religion in which the gods are not in conflict, where the omens remain ambiguous—since, in the last analysis, says the Socrates of Xenophon, it is the gods, not the birds, who foresee the future—where the divine reveals itself, like the *daimon* of Socrates, only by a silent warning and a reminder to man of his ignorance. Religion is, therefore, true, but true in a sense that it does not know—true as Socrates thinks it, not as it thinks.

And in the same way when he justifies the City, it is for his own reasons, not for *raisons d'Etat*. He does not run away. He appears before the tribunal. But there is little respect in the reasons he gives for this. First of all, he says, at my age the lust for life is not in place; furthermore, one would not put up with me much better elsewhere; finally, I have always lived here. There remains the celebrated argument for the authority of the laws. But we need to examine it more closely. Xenophon makes Socrates say that one may obey the laws in wishing for them to change, as one fights a war in wishing for peace. Thus it is not that the laws are good but that they pertain to order, and one needs order in order to change it. When Socrates refuses to flee, it is not that he recognizes the tribunal. It is that he may be in a better position to challenge it. By fleeing, that is, he would become an enemy of Athens and would make the sentence against him true. By remaining, he has won, whether he be acquitted or condemned, for he will prove his philosophy either in leading his judges to accept it, or in his own acceptance of the sentence.

Aristotle, seventy-five years later, will say, in leaving the city of his own accord, that there is no sense in allowing the Athenians to commit a new crime against philosophy. Socrates, on the other hand, works out for himself another idea of philosophy. It does not exist as a sort of idol of which he would be the guardian and which he must defend. It exists rather in its living relevance to the Athenians, in its absent presence, in its obedience without respect. Socrates has a way of obeying which is a way of resisting, while Aristotle disobeys in seemliness and dignity. Everything that Socrates does is ordered around the secret principle that one is annoyed if he does not comprehend. Always to blame by excess or default, always more simple and yet less abstract than the others, more flexible and less accommodating, he makes them ill at ease, and inflicts upon them the unpardonable offense of making them doubt themselves. He is there in life, at the assembly of the people, and before the tribunal, but in such a way that one can make nothing of him. He gives them no eloquence, no prepared rhetoric. By entering into the game of respect, he would only justify the calumny against him. But even less any show of defiance! This would be to forget that in a certain sense the others can hardly judge otherwise than they do. The same philosophy obliges him to appear before the judges and also makes him different from them. The same freedom which brings him among them frees him from their prejudices. The very same principle makes him both universal and singular. There is a part of him by which he is the kinsman of them all. It is called *reason* and is invisible to them. For them, as Aristophanes says, it is cloudy, empty chattering. The commentators sometimes say it is all a misunderstanding. Socrates believes in religion and the City, in spirit and in truth. They believe in them to the letter. He and his judges are not *on the same ground.* If only he had been better understood, one would have seen clearly that he was neither seeking for new gods, nor neglecting the gods of Athens. He was only trying to give them a sense; he was interpreting them.

The trouble is that this operation is not so innocent. It is in the world of the philosopher that one saves the gods and the laws by understanding them, and to make room on earth for the life of philosophy, it is precisely philosophers like Socrates who are required. Religion interpreted—this is for the others

religion suppressed. And the charge of impiety—
this is the point of view of the others towards him.
He gives reasons for obeying the laws. But it is already too much to have reasons for obeying, since
over against all reasons other reasons can be opposed, and then respect disappears. What one ex-
pects of him—this is exactly what he is not able to
give—is assent to the thing itself, without restric-
tion. He, on the contrary, comes before the judges,
yes, but it is to explain to them what the City is. As
if they did not know! As if they *were not* the City!
He does not plead for himself. He pleads the cause
of a city which would accept philosophy. He reverses
the roles and says to them: it is not myself I am
defending; it is you. In the last analysis the City is
in him and they are the enemies of the laws. It is
they who are being judged, and he who is judging
them—an inevitable reversal in the philosopher,
since he justifies what is outside by values which
come from within.

What can one do if he neither pleads his cause
nor challenges to combat? One can speak in such a
way as to make freedom show itself in and through
the various respects and considerations, and to un-
lock hate by a smile—a lesson for our philosophy
which has lost both its smile and its sense of tragedy.
This is what is called irony. The irony of Socrates
is a distant but true relation with others. It expresses the fundamental fact that each of us is only

himself inescapably, and nevertheless recognizes himself in the other. It is an attempt to open up both of us for freedom.[As is true of tragedy, both the adversaries are justified, and true irony uses a double-meaning which is founded on these facts.] There is therefore no self-conceit. It is irony on the self no less than on the others. As Hegel well says, it is *naive*. The irony of Socrates is not to say less in order to win an advantage in showing great mental power, or in suggesting some esoteric knowledge. "Whenever I convince anyone of his ignorance," the *Apology* says with melancholy, "my listeners imagine that I know everything that he does not know." Socrates does not know any *more* than they know. He knows only that there is no absolute knowledge, and that it is by this absence that we are open to the truth.

To this good irony Hegel opposes a romantic irony which is equivocal, tricky, and self-conceited. It relies on the power which we can use, if we wish, to give any kind of meaning to anything whatsoever. It levels things down; it plays with them and permits anything. The irony of Socrates is not this kind of madness. Or at least if there are traces of bad irony in it, it is Socrates himself who teaches us to correct Socrates. When he says: I make them dislike me and this is the proof that what I say is true, he is wrong on the basis of his own principles. All sound reasoning is offensive, but all that offends us is not true. At another time, when he says to his judges: I will not stop philosophizing *even if I must die many times,* he taunts them and tempts their cruelty. Sometimes it is clear that he yields to the giddiness of insolence and spitefulness, to self-magnification and the aristocratic spirit. He was left with no other resource than himself. As Hegel says again, he appeared "at the time of the decadence of the Athenian democracy; he drew away from the externally existent and retired into himself to seek there for the just and the good." But in the last analysis it was precisely this that he was self-prohibited from doing, since he thought that one cannot be just all alone and, indeed, that in being just all alone one ceases to be just. If it is truly the City that he is defending, it is not merely the City in him but that actual City existing around him. The five hundred men who gathered together to judge him were neither all important people nor all fools. Two hundred and twenty-one among them thought he was innocent, and a change of thirty votes would have saved Athens from the dishonor. It was also a question of those after Socrates who would run the same danger. He was perhaps free to bring down the anger of the fools upon himself, to pardon them with a certain contempt, and then to pass beyond his life. But this would not absolve him in advance from the evil he might bring on others and would not enable him to pass beyond *their* lives. It was therefore necessary to give to the tribunal its chance of understanding. In so far as we live with others, no judgment we make on them is possible which leaves us out, and which places them at a distance. *All is vain,* or *all is evil,* as likewise *all is well,* which are hard to distinguish, do not come from philosophy.

IV / Religion

⌊ IT IS POSSIBLE TO FEAR that our time also is rejecting the philosopher that dwells within it, and that once again philosophy will evaporate into nothing but *clouds.*⌋For to philosophize is to seek, and this is to imply that there are things to see and to say. Well, today we no longer seek. We "return" to one or the other of our traditions and "defend" it. Our convictions are founded less on perceived values and truths than on the vices and errors of those we do not like. We love very few things, though we dislike many. Our thinking is a thought in retreat or in reply. Each of us is expiating for his youth. This decadence is in accord with the course of our history. Having passed a certain point of tension, ideas cease to develop and live.⌊They fall to the level of justifications and pretexts, relics of the past, points of honor; and what one pompously calls the movement of ideas is reduced to the sum of our nostalgias, our grudges, our timidities, and our phobias.⌋ In this world, where negation and gloomy passion take the place of certitude, one does not seek above all to see, and, because it seeks to see, philosophy passes for impiety. It would be easy to show this in connection with two absolutes which are at the center of our discussions: God and history.

It is striking to find that today one no longer proves the existence of God, as Saint Thomas, Saint Anselm, and Descartes did. The proofs are ordinarily presupposed, and one limits one's self to refuting the negation of God either by seeking to find some gap in the new philosophies through which the constantly presupposed notion of the necessary being may be made to reappear or, if these philosophies place this notion decidedly in question, by abruptly disqualifying them as *atheism*. Even such relatively serene reflections as those of Father de Lubac on atheistic humanism, and those of M. Maritain on the meaning of contemporary atheism are carried on as if philosophy, when it is not theological, is reduced to the negation of God. Father de Lubac takes as the object of his study an atheism which truly wishes, he says, "to replace what it destroys," which, therefore, begins by destroying what it wishes to replace, and which is rather, like that of Nietzsche, a sort of deicide. Maritain examines what he rather curiously calls positive atheism, and which soon comes to appear to him as an "active combat against everything that suggests God," an "antitheism," an "act of inverted faith," a "refusal of God," a "defiance against God." This antitheism certainly exists, but since it is an inverted theology, it is not a philosophy, and by focusing the whole discussion on it, one shows perhaps that it holds locked up within itself the very theology it is attacking. But at the same time one reduces everything to a controversy between theism and anthropotheism as they re-echo the troubles of religious alienation, and forgets to ask whether the philosopher really has to choose either the theology and the apocalypse of Wonderland or the "mystique of the superman," and whether any philosopher has ever endowed man with the metaphysical functions of omnipotence.

Philosophy works itself out in another order, and it is for the same reasons that it eludes both Promethean humanism and the rival affirmations of theology. The philosopher does not say that a final transcendence of human contradictions may be possible, and that the complete man awaits us in the future. Like everyone else, he knows nothing of this. He says—and this is something altogether different —that the world is going on, that we do not have to judge its future by what has happened in the past, that the idea of a destiny in things is not an idea but a dizziness, that our relations with nature are not fixed once and for all, that no one can know what freedom may be able to do, nor imagine what our customs and human relations would be in a civilization no longer haunted by competition and necessity. He does not place his hope in any destiny, even a favorable one, but in something belonging to us which is precisely not a destiny—in the contingency of our history. The denial of this is a fixed (non-philosophical) position.

Must we then say that the philosopher is a humanist? No, if one understands by "man" an explanatory principle which ought to be substituted for the others. One explains nothing by man, since he is not a force but a weakness at the heart of being, a cosmological factor, but also the place where all cosmological factors, by a mutation which is never finished, change in sense and become history. Man is as effective in the contemplation of an inhuman nature as in the love of himself. His existence extends to too many things, in fact to all, for him to become the object of his own delight, or for the authorization of what we can now reasonably call a "human chauvinism." This same wide-ranging flexibility, which eludes every religion of humanity, also takes the wind from the sails of theology. For theology recognizes the contingency of human existence only to derive it from a necessary being, that is, to remove it. Theology makes use of philosophical wonder only for the purpose of motivating an affirmation which ends it. Philosophy, on the other hand, arouses us to what is problematic in our own existence and in that of the world, to such a point that

we shall never be cured of searching for a solution,
as Bergson says, "in the notebooks of the master."

Father de Lubac discusses an atheism which
means to suppress this searching, he says, "even including the problem as to what is responsible for the
birth of God in human consciousness." This problem
is so little ignored by the philosopher that, on the
contrary, he radicalizes it, and places it above the
"solutions" which stifle it. [The idea of necessary
being, as well as that of "eternal matter" and "total
man," appear prosaic to him in comparison with
this constant manifesting of religious phenomena
through all the stages of world history, and this con-
tinual rebirth of the divine which he is trying to
describe. [In this situation, he is well able to understand religion as one of the expressions of the central phenomenon of consciousness.] But the example
of Socrates reminds us that it is not the same thing,
but almost the opposite, to understand religion and
to accept it. Lichtenberg, of whom Kant said that
each of his phrases hid a profound thought, held
something of the following kind: one should neither
affirm the existence of God nor deny it. As he ex-
plained: "it is not necessary that doubt should be
anything more than vigilance; otherwise, it can become a source of danger." It is not that he wished
merely to leave certain perspectives open, nor to
please everyone. It is rather that he was identifying
himself, for his part, with a consciousness of self, of

the world, and of others that was "strange" (the word is his) in a sense which is equally well destroyed by the rival explanations.

[This decisive moment when certain particles of matter, words, and events allow themselves to be animated by a meaning, the nearest contours of which they suggest without containing, is above all the fundamental keynote of the world which is already given with the least of our perceptions.] Both consciousness and history echo this. It is the same thing to establish them against any naturalistic explanation as it is to release them from any sovereign necessity. Hence one bypasses philosophy when one *defines* it as atheism. This is philosophy as it is seen by the theologian. Its negation is only the beginning of an attention, a seriousness, an experience on the basis of which it must be judged. Furthermore, if one remembers the history of the word *atheism,* and how it has been applied even to Spinoza, the most positive of philosophers, we must admit that all thinking which displaces, or otherwise defines, the sacred has been called atheistic, and that philosophy which does not place it here or there, like a thing, but at the joining of things and words, will always be exposed to this reproach without ever being touched by it.

A sensitive and open thought should not fail to guess that there is an affirmative meaning and even a presence of the spirit in this philosophical negativity. Indeed Maritain finally comes to justify the continuous criticism of idols as essential to Christianity. The saint, he says, is a "complete atheist" with respect to a God who would be only the guarantor of the natural order, who would consecrate not only all the world's goodness but all the world's evil as well, who would justify slavery, injustice, the tears of children, the agony of the innocent by sacred necessities, who would finally sacrifice man to the cosmos as "the absurd Emperor of the world." The Christian God who redeems the world and is accessible to prayer, according to Maritain, is the active negation of all this. Here, indeed, we are close to the essence of Christianity. The philosopher will only ask himself if the natural and rational concept of God as necessary being is not inevitably that of the Emperor of the world, if without this concept, the Christian God would not cease to be the author of the world, and if the criticism we are now suggesting is not the philosophy which presses to the limit that criticism of false gods which Christianity has introduced into our history? Yes, *where* will one stop the criticism of idols, and *where* will one ever be able to say the true God actually resides if, as Maritain writes, we pay tribute to false gods "every time we bow before the world"?

V / History

In considering the other theme of contemporary discussion, history, one may see that here again philosophy seems to despair of itself. Some see in history an external destiny for the sake of which the philosopher is invited to suppress himself as philosopher. Others maintain that philosophy is autonomous, but only by detaching it from concrete circumstances, and by making of it an honorable alibi. One *defends* philosophy and one *defends* history as though they were rival traditions. The founders who lived these traditions found no great difficulty in bringing them to coexist in themselves. For taken in their original condition, in human practice, they do not divide into opposed alternatives. They advance and decline together.

Hegel had already identified them, by making philosophy the understanding of historical experience, and history the becoming of philosophy. But the conflict was only masked, since for Hegel philosophy is absolute knowledge, system, totality, whereas the history of which the philosopher speaks is not really history, that is to say, something which one does. It is rather universal history, fully comprehended, finished, dead. But, on the other hand, history as pure fact or event, introduces into the system in which it is incorporated an internal movement which tears it to pieces. These two points of view both remain true for Hegel, and we know that he carefully maintained this equivocation. At certain times he makes the philosopher appear as the simple reader of a history already accomplished, as the owl of Minerva who takes flight only at dusk, when the work of history is finished. But at other times he seems to make the philosopher the only subject of history, since he alone does not undergo it, but comprehends it by elevating it to the level of the concept. In reality this equivocation works to the profit of the philosopher. [Since history has been staged by him, he finds in it only the sense he has already placed there, and in accepting it he merely accepts himself.] It is to Hegel, perhaps, that we should apply what Alain has said of the subtler merchants of sleep who "offer us a sleep in which the dreams are precisely the world in which we live." The universal history of Hegel is the dream of history. As in our dreams, all that is thought is real, and all that is real is thought. There is nothing at all for men to do who are not already taken up in the system. The philosopher does in fact make a certain concession to them. He admits that he is not able to think of anything that has not already been done, thus granting to them the monopoly of efficient action. But since he reserves the monopoly of meaning to himself, it is in the philosopher, and in him alone, that history makes sense. It is the philosopher who thinks and who decrees the identity of history and philosophy —which is to say in other words that there is no such thing.

The novelty of Marx, as a critic of Hegel, was, therefore, not to identify the mover of history with human productivity, nor to interpret philosophy as a reflection of historical movement, but rather to denounce the trick by which the philosopher slips the system into history in order then to recover it and to reaffirm its omnipotence precisely at the moment when he seemed to give it up. Even the privilege of speculative philosophy, the claim of philosophical existence, as the young Marx said, to take up all the other forms of existence, is itself a historical fact, not the bringing to birth of history. Marx himself discovers a historical rationality immanent in the life of men. For him, history is not merely the order of fact or of reality on which philosophy, with its rationality, will confer the right to exist. History is rather the situation in which all meanings are developed, and in particular the conceptual meanings of philosophy, in so far as they are legitimate. What Marx calls *praxis* is the meaning which works itself out spontaneously in the intercrossing of those activities by which man organizes his relations with nature and with other men. It is not directed at the beginning by an idea of universal or total history. We must remember that Marx insisted on the impossibility of thinking the future. It is rather the analysis of the past and present which enables us to perceive in outline a logic in the course of things which does not so much guide it from the outside as emanate from within it, and which will be achieved only if men understand their experience, and will to change it. From the course of things we know only that sooner or later it will eliminate the irrational historical forms which secrete ferments that will destroy them. This elimination of the irrational can lead to chaos, if the forces destroying these forms do not show themselves capable of constructing something new out of them. Hence there is no universal history. Perhaps we shall never advance beyond pre-history. Historical meaning is immanent in the interhuman event, and is as fragile as this event. But precisely because of this, the event takes on the value of a genesis of reason. Philosophy no longer has the power of exhaustive comprehension which Hegel gave it. But also it can no longer be, as with Hegel, the mere reflection of a history that is past. As the young Marx said at another time, one "destroys" philosophy as a detached mode of knowing, only to "realize" it in actual history. Rationality passes from the concept to the heart of interhuman *praxis*, and certain historical facts take on a metaphysical meaning. Philosophy lives in these facts.

In denying to philosophical thought the power of

exhaustive comprehension, Marx is not able, as his
successors and perhaps he himself believed, to turn
the dialectic of consciousness into a dialectic of matter, or things. When a man says that there is a dialectic in things, this can mean only in things so far
as he thinks them, and such objectivity, as the example of Hegel shows, is the height of subjectivism.
Marx, therefore, does not transfer the dialectic into
things; he transforms it into men, understood of
course with all their human equipment as being engaged, through work and culture, in an enterprise
which transforms nature and social relations. Philosophy is not an illusion. It is the algebra of history.
Furthermore, the contingency of human events is no
longer understood as a defect in the logic of history,
but rather as its condition. Without such contingency
there would be only a phantom of history. If one
knows where history is going inevitably, events
taken one by one have neither importance nor meaning. The future is already ripe, whatever happens.
Nothing is truly at stake in the present, since whatever it may be, it is proceeding towards the same
future. On the contrary, whoever thinks that there
is something preferable in the present implies that
the future is contingent. History has no meaning, if
this meaning is understood as that of a river which,
under the influence of all-powerful causes, flows
towards an ocean in which it disappears. Every ap-
peal to universal history cuts off the meaning of the

specific event, renders effective history insignificant, and is a nihilism in disguise. As an external God is *ipso facto* a false God, so an external history is no longer history. The two rival absolutes live only if, in full being, a human project which challenges them is opened up. It is in history that philosophy learns to know this philosophical negativity, to which one vainly opposes the finished completeness of history.

If the followers of Marx hardly understood him, and if he himself, after his youthful writings, ceased to understand himself in this way, it was because his original insight into *praxis* put in question the usual categories of philosophy, and because nothing in sociology and in positive history was preparing the way for the intellectual reform which he called for. Where, in fact, was this immanent meaning of inter-human events to be placed? It is not, or certainly it is not always, in men, that is, in their minds, but outside them. Once we had stopped placing any absolute knowledge in things, it seemed that there were only blind events. *Where* then was the historical process, and what mode of existence must be recognized in such historical forms as feudalism, capitalism, proletariat, which are spoken of as though they were persons, knowing and willing, hidden behind the multiplicity of events, without seeing clearly what these masks [*prosopopées*] represent? After rejecting the expedient of the Hegelian Objective Spirit, how could the dilemma of existence as thing versus existence as consciousness be avoided? How could one understand the generalized meaning which works in these historical forms and in the whole of history, which is not the thought of any one mind but which appeals to all? The simplest possibility was to imagine vaguely a dialectic of matter, whereas Marx, on the contrary, spoke of a "human matter," held, that is, in the movement of *praxis*. But this expedient altered the intuition of Marx. In relation to the dialectic of things, all philosophy fell to the rank of ideology, illusion, or even of mystification. One lost all means of knowing whether, as Marx intended, philosophy was finally realized in its destruction, or whether it was simply made to disappear—to say nothing of the injuries suffered by the concept of history.

As often happens with philosophical insights, the union of philosophy and history lives again in more recent and special investigations which, though not directly inspired by Hegel and Marx, retrace their steps because they confront the very same difficulties. The theory of signs, as developed in linguistics, perhaps implies a conception of historical meaning which gets beyond the opposition of *things* versus *consciousness*. Living language is precisely that togetherness of thinking and thing which causes the difficulty. In the act of speaking, the subject, in his tone and in his style, bears witness to his autonomy, since nothing is more proper to him, and yet at the same moment, and without contradiction, he is turned towards the linguistic community and is dependent on his language. The will to speak is one and the same as the will to be understood. The presence of the individual in the institution, and of the institution in the individual is evident in the case of linguistic change. It is often the wearing down of a form which suggests to us a new way of using the means of discrimination which are present in the language at a given time. The constant need for communication leads us to invent and to accept a new usage which is not deliberate and yet which is systematic. The contingent fact, taken over by the will to expression, becomes a new means of expression which takes its place, and has a lasting sense in the history of this language. In such cases, there is a rationality in the contingent, a lived logic, a self-constitution of which we have definite need in trying to understand the union of contingency and meaning in history, and Sassure, the modern linguist, could have sketched a new philosophy of history.

The reciprocal relations between the will to express and the means of expression correspond to those between the productive forces and the forms of production, and more generally, between historical forces and institutions. Just as language is a system of signs which have meaning only in relation to one another, and each of which has its own usage throughout the whole language, so each institution is a symbolic system that the subject takes over and incorporates as a style of functioning, as a global configuration, without having any need to conceive it at all. When equilibrium is destroyed, the reorganizations which take place comprise, like those of language, an internal logic even though it may not be clearly thought out by anyone. They are polarized by the fact that, as participants in a system of symbols, we exist in the eyes of one another, with one another, in such a way that changes in language are due to our will to speak and to be understood. The system of symbols affects the molecular changes which occur where a meaning develops, a meaning which is neither a thing nor an idea, in spite of the famous dichotomy, because it is a modulation of our coexistence. It is in this way, as is also true of logics of behavior, that the forms and processes of history, the classes, the epochs, exist. We were asking ourselves where they are. They are in a social, cultural, or symbolic space which is no less real than physical space and is, moreover, supported by it. For meaning lies latent not only in language, in political and religious institutions, but in modes of kinship, in machines, in the landscape, in production, and, in general, in all the modes of human commerce. An interconnection among all these phenomena is possible, since they are all symbolisms, and perhaps even the translation of one symbolism into another is possible.

What is the situation of philosophy with respect to a history thus conceived? Each philosophy is also an architecture of signs. It constitutes itself in close relation with the other modes of exchange which make up our historical and social life. Philosophy is in history, and is never independent of historical discourse. But for the tacit symbolism of life it substitutes, in principle, a conscious symbolism; for a latent meaning, one that is manifest. It is never content to accept its historical situation (as it is not content to accept its own past). It changes this situation by revealing it to itself and, therefore, by giving it the opportunity of entering into conversation with other times and other places where its truth appears. Hence it is no more possible to set up a one-to-one correspondence between the historical event and the conscious philosophical interpretations of this event, than between the event and its objective conditions. The book, if it is authentic, transcends itself as a dated event. Philosophical, aesthetic, and literary criticism, therefore, have an intrinsic value, and history can never take their place. It is also true, however, that one can always recover from the book the fragments of history on which it has crystallized, and this is really necessary in order to know to what extent it has changed them in their truth. Philosophy turns towards the anonymous symbolic activity from which we emerge, and towards the personal discourse which develops in us, and which, indeed, we are. It scrutinizes this power of expression which the other forms of symbolism exercise only in a limited way. In touch with every kind of fact and experience, it tries rigorously to grasp those fecund moments in which a meaning takes possession of itself. It recovers this meaning, and also pushes beyond all limits the becoming of truth, which presupposes and brings it about that there is only one history and one world.

VI / Philosophy

Let us show, in conclusion, that views like these justify philosophy even in its weakness.

For it is useless to deny that philosophy limps. It dwells in history and in life, but it wishes to dwell at their center, at the point where they come into being with the birth of meaning. It is not content with what is already there. Since it is expression in act, it comes to itself only by ceasing to coincide with what is expressed, and by taking its distance in order to see its meaning. It is, in fact, the Utopia of possession at a distance. Hence it can be tragic, since it has its own contrary within itself. It is never a *serious* occupation. The serious man, if he exists, is the man of one thing only, to which he assents. But the most resolute philosophers always wish the contrary—to realize, but in destroying; to suppress, but also to conserve. Always, they have an afterthought. The philosopher pays attention to the serious man— of action, of religion, or of passion—perhaps more acutely than anyone. But precisely in doing this, one feels that he is different. His own actions are acts of witness, like the "signifying acts" by which the companions of Julien Sorel at the seminary sought to prove their piety. Spinoza writes *"ultimi barbarorum"* on the tyrants' gate. Lagneau took legal action before the University authorities to rehabilitate an unfortunate candidate. Having done these things, each returns home, and remains there for years. The philosopher of action is perhaps the farthest removed from action, for to speak of action with depth and rigor is to say that one does not desire to act.

Machiavelli is the complete contrary of a machiavellian, since he describes the tricks of power and, as we say, "gives the whole show away." The seducer and the politician, who live in the dialectic and have a feeling or instinct for it, try their best to keep it hidden. It is the philosopher who explains that dialectically, under given conditions, an opponent becomes the equivalent of a traitor. This language is the precise opposite of what the powers say. The powers omit the premises and speak more succinctly. They simply say: here there are nothing but criminals. The manichees, who throw themselves into action, understand one another better than they understand the philosopher, for there is a certain complicity among them. Each one is the reason for the being of the other. But the philosopher is a stranger to this fraternal melée. Even if he had never betrayed any cause, one feels, in his very manner of being faithful, that he would be able to betray. He does not take sides like the others, and in his assent something massive and carnal is lacking. He is not altogether a real being.

This difference exists. But is it really between the philosopher and the man? It is rather the difference in man himself between that which understands and that which chooses, and every man, like the philosopher, is divided in this way. There is much that is artificial in the portrait of the man of action whom we oppose to the philosopher. This man of action is himself not all of one piece. Hate is a virtue from behind. To obey with one's eyes closed is the beginning of panic; and to choose against what one understands, the beginning of skepticism. One must be able to withdraw and gain distance in order to become truly engaged, which is, also, always an engagement in the truth. The same author who wrote one day that all action is manichean, having become involved in action soon after, familiarly answered a journalist who reminded him of what he had said: "all action is manichean, *but don't overdo it!*"

No one is manichean before himself. It is an air that men of action have when seen from the outside, and which they rarely treasure in their memories.

If the philosopher helps us to understand, hence-forth, something of what a great man says in his own heart, he saves the truth for all, even for the man of action, who needs it, for no real statesman has ever seriously said that he was not interested in the truth. Later on, perhaps tomorrow, the man of action will rehabilitate the philosopher. As for those who are simply men, and not professionals in action, they are very far from classifying all others into the good and the evil, at least as long as they speak of what they have seen, and judge from close up. One finds them, when one looks, to be surprisingly sensi-tive to philosophical irony, as if it brought their si-lence and their reserve into the light, because here, for once, the word serves to open and release us.

The limping of philosophy is its virtue. True irony is not an alibi; it is a task; and the very detachment of the philosopher assigns to him a certain kind of action among men. Because we live in one of those situations that Hegel called diplomatic, in which every initiative risks being changed in meaning, we sometimes believe that we are serving the cause of philosophy by isolating it from the problems of the day, and Descartes has recently been honored for not having taken sides between Galileo and the Holy Office. The philosopher, it is said, should not prefer one rival dogmatism to another. He should occupy himself with absolute being beyond both the object of the physicist and the imagination of the theologian. But this is to forget that, by refusing to speak, Descartes also refuses to vindicate and to bring into action the philosophical order in its proper place. By remaining silent, he does not transcend these twin errors. He leaves them at grips with one another; he encourages them, particularly the victor of the moment. [To be silent is not the same as to say why one does not wish to choose] If Descartes had acted, he could not have failed to establish the relative right of Galileo against the Holy Office, even if this were finally to subordinate ontology to physics. [Philosophy and absolute being are never above the rival errors that oppose each other at any given time.] These are never errors in quite the same way, and philosophy, which is integral truth, is charged with saying what in them it is able to integrate. In order that one day there might be a state of the world in which free thought would be possible, of scientism as well as of imagination, it did not suffice to bypass these two errors in silence. It was essential to speak against, and in this case to speak against the imagination. In the case of Galileo, the thought of physics carried the interests of truth. The philosophical absolute does not have any permanent seat. It is never elsewhere; it must be defended in each event. Alain said to his students: "Truth is momentary for us men who have a short view. It belongs to a situation, to an instant; it is necessary to see it, to say it, to do it at this very moment, not before nor after in ridiculous maxims; not for many times, for there are no many times." The difference here is not between the man and the philosopher. Both of them think the truth in the event. They are both opposed to the important one who thinks by principles, and against the roué who lives without truth.

At the conclusion of a reflection which at first isolates him, the philosopher, in order to experience more fully the ties of truth which bind him to the world and history, finds neither the depth of himself nor absolute knowledge, but a renewed image of the world and of himself placed within it among others. His dialectic, or his ambiguity, is only a way of putting into words what every man knows well— the value of those moments when his life renews itself and continues on, when he gets hold of himself again, and understands himself by passing beyond, when his private world becomes the common world. These mysteries are in each one of us as in him. What does he say of the relation between the soul and the body, except what is known by all men who make their souls and bodies, their good and their evil, go together in one piece? What does he teach of death, except that it is hidden in life, as the body in the soul, and that it is this understanding, as Montaigne said, which brings "a peasant and whole peoples to die, just as surely as philosophers?" The philosopher is the man who wakes up and speaks. And man contains silently within himself

the paradoxes of philosophy, because to be completely a man, it is necessary to be a little more and a
little less than man.

Author's Notes

NOTE I

This double movement can be noted in his reflections on death and immortality—problems, he
thought, which put to the test all our analyses of the
relation between mind and the world. Lavelle was
opposed to conceptions which would make of death a
simple break between life in the relative and life in
the absolute, and of immortality, a prolonging of
life, or, as he said, the "tomorrow after death." When
he spoke of immortality, he did not say that death is
nothing and that life continues after it, but, on the
contrary, that by death the subject passes into another mode of being. Freed from dispersion and alienation, concentrated in himself, changed in essence, he is, for the first time, fully that which he
has never been able to be, except imperfectly. Life
was, therefore, a sort of deficient eternity, the seal
of the eternal being stamped only on a terminated
existence. Life was the vigil of death. Indeed, in
certain passages of *l'Ame humaine,* the terminal
event is "incorporated in our souls." Death gives "to

all events which precede it that mark of the absolute which they would never possess if they were not going to be suddenly interrupted." The absolute inhabits each of our enterprises, in so far as it is done once and for all, and will never begin again. It comes to our life in virtue of its very temporality. Thus the eternal becomes fluid, and flows back from the end into the heart of life. Death is no longer the truth of life, and life is no longer the waiting for that moment when we will be changed in our essence. What is always unfinished, deficient, and cramped in the present is no longer a sign of a lesser reality. But, then, the truth of a being is not its essence, or what it has finally become. It is rather its existence, its active becoming. And if, as Lavelle used to say, we believe ourselves to be closer to the dead we have loved than to the living, this is because they no longer place us in question, and because, from now on, we can dream of them as we choose. Such piety is not far from being impious. The only memory which respects them is the one which maintains the actual use they have made of themselves and of their world, the accent of their freedom in the incompleteness of their lives. The same fragile principle makes us alive, and also gives to what we do a sense that does not wear out.

NOTE II

It must be noted even now that instead of a dialectic of time and space, in Bergson it is often a question of a sort of contamination of time by space, as when he speaks of "attributing material extension to perception." The truth is that one never knows whether Bergson is bringing *durée* down into matter and relaxing it in such a way as to destroy it as *durée,* or whether he is making of matter, and of the world, a system of symbols in which the *durée* realizes itself. His thought is not clear on this point, because he did not see the two alternatives. Assuming a "super-consciousness" as the source of both matter and consciousness, he believed he was justified in saying that matter is "like a consciousness where everything is in balance." The strange solidarity of space and *durée,* of things and consciousness, which he found in us, was only the result of their common origin. As for us, we receive their mediation already fully accomplished. Having accepted the paradox of an external expression of the spirit once and for all, and even before we appear on the scene, we need only to describe *extension,* as Bergson says in a significant phrase, "without further scruples." It is precisely under cover of this cosmology that Bergson was able to develop his intuition of the concrete relations between the *durée* and space, spirit and body, without perceiving that this makes the idea of a super-consciousness, or a bodiless spirit, very difficult. In this manner, his philosophy conceals from itself the very problem on the basis of which it was constructed.

NOTE III

It is true that this reading of a life which, as he said of painting, "speaks to our intelligence," led Bergson, before long, to consider it as unmediated. He thought that the painter is himself at the center of his work, and that he possesses "the secret of its physiognomy," although, like all those who struggle with a language, and even more those who create one, the painter does not understand himself as the organizing law of his acts. Bergson was wrong in believing that the picture is "a simple act projected on the canvas," since it is rather the sedimented result of a series of expressive efforts. Without doubt, for him, the phenomenology of life would have been only a preface to the explanation of life by consciousness.